YORK NOTES

KS2 ENGLISH SATS

3-STEP TEST BOOSTER: GRAMMAR, PUNCTUATION AND SPELLING

HELEN CHILTON

YORK PRESS
322 Old Brompton Road, London SW5 9JH

PEARSON EDUCATION LIMITED
Edinburgh Gate, Harlow,
Essex CM20 2JE, United Kingdom
Associated companies, branches and representatives throughout the world

First published 2018

10 9 8 7 6 5 4 3 2 1

ISBN 978–1–2922–3284–3

Typeset by Ken Vail Graphic Design Ltd
Printed in the UK.

Image credits: Anonymous/Open Clip Art for page 5 and elsewhere; monstergraingames/Open Clip Art for page 27 and elsewhere; Merlin2525/Open Clip Art for page 27 and elsewhere

CONTENTS

Section C: 30-minute tests

Answers

Record your progress!

HOW TO USE YOUR *3-STEP TEST BOOSTER: GRAMMAR, PUNCTUATION AND SPELLING* BOOK

Getting up to speed for the Key Stage 2 English grammar, punctuation and spelling tests is as easy as 1 – 2 – 3 with this fantastic *3-Step Test Booster: Grammar, Punctuation and Spelling* book!

Before you begin, carefully pull out the spelling test scripts on pages 43–46, or ask an adult to help you. Give them to your parent, carer or teacher.

Test yourself in three easy steps:

STEP ONE – 10-minute tests
Quick tests to get you off to a good start!

STEP TWO – 20-minute tests
Longer tests to build your skills and stamina!

STEP THREE – 30-minute tests
Extended practice to ensure you're ready for your Key Stage 2 test!

TOP TEST TIPS
- Time yourself or work at your own speed.
- Use the Answers at the back to get your scores.
- Record your scores with the handy Scorecards and Progress chart.
- See your skills and confidence grow!

Good luck and enjoy!

1 Which sentence uses **capital letters** correctly?

Tick **one**.

On tuesday James and I went swimming at
the new pool in the centre of London.

☐

On Tuesday James and I went swimming at
the new pool in the centre of London.

☐

on Tuesday james and i went swimming at
the new pool in the centre of London.

☐

On tuesday James and I went swimming at
the new pool in the centre of london.

☐

1 mark

2 What is the **function** of the sentence below?

What an amazing bike

Tick **one**.

question   ☐

command   ☐

exclamation   ☐

statement   ☐

1 mark

3 Read the sentences below. Circle the **three verbs** in the **simple present tense**.

My friend Mike always comes round to my house on Friday nights.

We watch a film or play computer games.

---
1 mark

4 Circle the **three conjunctions** in the sentence below.

I told Dad I'd ring him when football practice finished, so he could

come and pick me up.

---
1 mark

5 Read the sentences below.
Tick **two** sentences that **use the correct tenses.**

Tick **two**.

I learned French since September.	☐
By the time Dad got home from work, we'd already eaten our dinner.	☐
I was going to Paul's house later because it will be his birthday.	☐
The school bus usually picks us up at ten past eight.	☐

---
1 mark

6 Which sentence uses **commas** correctly?

Tick **one**.

My favourite, snacks are chocolate, crisps, nuts, and ice cream. ☐

My favourite snacks are chocolate, crisps, nuts and ice cream. ☐

My favourite snacks are, chocolate, crisps, nuts, and ice cream. ☐

My favourite snacks, are chocolate, crisps, nuts and ice cream. ☐

———
1 mark

7 Circle the **three determiners** in the sentence below.

It took ages to find a good place to have the picnic, but eventually

we found an old wall to sit on.

———
1 mark

8 Draw a line to match each sentence to the missing **relative pronoun**.

Sentence   **Relative pronoun**

The girls, _____ go to dance class
together every Saturday, became great friends.   whose

I'm going to have a strawberry ice
cream, _____ is my favourite flavour.   who

That's the boy _____ father was
a famous rock star in the 1990s.   which

———
1 mark

9 Draw a line to match each adjective with its **antonym**.

Adjective	Antonym
lucky	mean
special	unfortunate
generous	ordinary

1 mark

10 Rewrite the sentence below. Include two **apostrophes**.

This is Arjuns poster and those are the other students posters.

_____

_____

1 mark

Well done for completing this test! Add up your marks and work out your total score.

TOTAL SCORE: .... (out of 10)

GRAMMAR AND PUNCTUATION
TEST 2

1 Draw a line to match each sentence with the correct **punctuation**. Use each punctuation mark only **once**.

Sentence   **Punctuation mark**

What an amazing house   .

Our house isn't very big   ?

Has your house got a garden   !

1 mark

2 What is the **function** of the sentence below?

Sit down and listen, everyone

Tick **one**.

statement ☐

question ☐

command ☐

exclamation ☐

1 mark

3 Which word is the **adverb** in the sentence below?

I'm going camping with my family soon.

Tick **one**.

camping ☐

my ☐

soon ☐

4 Circle the **two verbs** in this sentence.

I play netball with my friends on Saturdays and visit my grandparents on Sundays.

5 Which sentence uses the **past progressive tense**?

Tick **one**.

I've been enjoying the book a lot. ☐

I was playing in the garden when Mum called me in for dinner. ☐

I'd been swimming for two hours and I was really tired. ☐

6 Circle the **semi-colon** in this text.

Poppy didn't get home until late; her bus didn't turn up on time. She had two options: start walking or wait. She decided to wait and then three buses all came at once!

7 Which **prefix** can be added to **every** word below to give the **opposite meaning**?

even

helpful

kind

tidy

successful

Tick **one**.

mis-	☐
re-	☐
un-	☐
dis-	☐

8 Which sentence uses **commas** correctly?

Tick **one**.

Ben's new dog which his family brought home at the weekend, has settled in well. ☐

Ben's new dog, which his family brought home at the weekend has settled in well. ☐

Ben's new dog, which his family brought home at the weekend, has settled in well. ☐

Ben's new dog which his family brought home at the weekend, has settled in, well. ☐

1 mark

9 Circle the **noun phrase** in this sentence.

The lazy old cat lay on the mat while the fire burned brightly.

1 mark

10 Complete the sentences below with the **past simple** form of the verb *be*.

Sorry I _____ not at home when you called yesterday.
(was/were)

I _____ out with my parents. We _____ at the
(was/were)   (was/were)

supermarket for hours!

1 mark

Well done for completing this test! Add up your marks and work out your total score.

TOTAL SCORE: .... (out of 10)

1 Which **punctuation** is shown below, not including the colon and full stop?

Things you will need for the trip:

- a bottle of water
- comfortable walking boots
- a map of the area.

Tick **one**.

dashes ☐

brackets ☐

bullet points ☐

semi-colons ☐

1 mark

2 Circle the **subject** in the sentence below.

Maria took the dog for a walk before school.

1 mark

3 Circle the **subordinate clause** in the sentence below.

Jake's birthday presents, which were sitting neatly wrapped on the

table, had cost his parents a lot of money.

1 mark

4 Read the **hyphenated** sentence below. Then tick the correct the meaning of the sentence.

My Dad often works twenty-four-hour shifts.

Tick **one**.

My Dad often works 24 shifts which last one hour. ☐

My Dad often works shifts which last 24 hours. ☐

My Dad often works 20 shifts which last four hours. ☐

1 mark

5 Which **punctuation mark** should be used in the place shown by the arrow?

Please wash your hands

↑

Tick **one**.

comma ☐

full stop ☐

exclamation mark ☐

question mark ☐

1 mark

6 Look at the sentences containing **modal verbs**. How certain is it that the events will happen? Tick the correct box.

	Certain	Not certain
I might go to Jude's party at the weekend.		
Isaac will meet you at the corner in ten minutes.		
It may rain later so take an umbrella with you.		

1 mark

7 Circle the words which could go in **brackets** in the sentence below.

The trainers Oliver wanted Star Brand were out of stock.

8 Draw a line to match each word to the **correct suffix**.
Use each suffix **once**. The first one has been done for you.

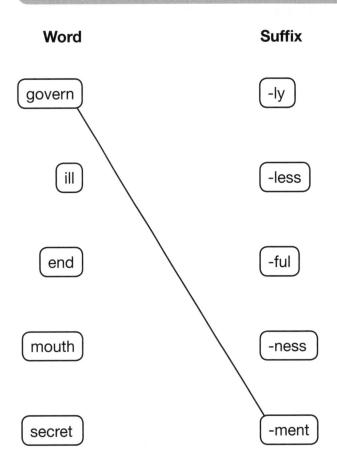

Word	Suffix
govern	-ly
ill	-less
end	-ful
mouth	-ness
secret	-ment

1 mark

9 Tick the sentence which uses the **present perfect tense**.

Tick **one**.

I've been playing XCars all morning. It's a brilliant game! ☐

I didn't learn to swim until I was eleven. ☐

Have you ever been to Thornly theme park? ☐

Leon and Eva were walking the dog when they found the money. ☐

1 mark

10 Read the sentences below and write the missing **relative pronouns** in the correct spaces.

who   which   whose

a. Do you know _____ bag that is? Is it Charlotte's?

b. Do you mean the one _____ is hanging on the back of the

chair? Sorry, I don't know _____ it belongs to.

1 mark

Well done for completing this test! Add up your marks and work out your total score.

TOTAL SCORE: .... (out of 10)

GRAMMAR AND PUNCTUATION
TEST 4

1   What is the **function** of the sentence below?

What have you been doing all afternoon

Tick **one**.

command ☐

question ☐

statement ☐

exclamation ☐

1 mark

2   Circle the **colon** in this sentence.

I bought a lot of snacks to eat during the film: popcorn, sweets and

nachos – Mum said I was greedy!

1 mark

3   Circle the **three prepositions** in the sentence below.

After swimming, we had a milkshake at the café before we

went home.

1 mark

4 Which of the following sentences contains a **plural possessive pronoun**?

Tick **one**.

The red car is ours. ☐

The small fluffy cat is hers. ☐

The dog is sitting in its kennel. ☐

This isn't my laptop – it's his. ☐

_____
1 mark

5 Use the **suffixes** to make adjectives. Use each suffix **twice**.

| -ful |

| -less |

play_____

home_____

end_____

wonder_____

_____
1 mark

6 Circle the **incorrect verb form** in the sentence below.

Danny had cooked his parents' dinner by the time they have got

home. They said it was the best meal they'd ever had!

1 mark

7 Tick **two** sentences which contain **parenthesis**.

Tick **two**.

Erin (my older sister) is really good on the guitar. ⬜

I'm so thirsty – I could drink a whole bottle of cola! ⬜

The cake – which looked great – wasn't as tasty as I'd hoped. ⬜

1 mark

8 Identify the **main clause** and **subordinate clause** in the sentence below.
Write **Main** or **Sub** in the boxes.

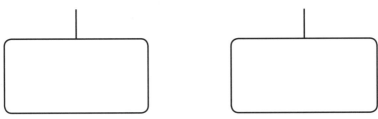

After we've been to the cinema, Dad's going to take us for a pizza.

1 mark

SECTION A: GRAMMAR AND PUNCTUATION TEST 4

9 Add the missing **punctuation** to the sentence below.

I don't know where your glasses are said Jo

_____
1 mark

10 Circle the **three progressive verb forms** in the text below.

I'm sitting by my bedroom window, and I can see our neighbours in their garden. Their little boy, Jules, is playing with a ball and his parents are reading.

_____
1 mark

Well done for completing this test! Add up your marks and work out your total score.

TOTAL SCORE: .... (out of 10)

SPELLING TEST

1. My best _____ Connor is really good at gymnastics.

2. I love _____ stories – you never know what will happen!

3. We had _____ getting tickets for the match.

4. "_____, my name's Tegan, not Joanna," said the girl.

5. The pirates found the _____ on the beach.

6. Hannah got her favourite footballer's _____ after the match.

7. For the special _____, Sonja bought a new dress.

8. The teacher gave an _____ of the solar system.

9. Luke was _____ that he was looking quite scruffy.

10. My _____ is having a party at the weekend.

11. Scientists wonder about the _____ of life on other planets.

12. The _____ ran backwards and forwards along the pitch.

Well done for completing this test! Add up your marks and work out your total score.

TOTAL SCORE: .... (out of 12)

SECTION A: SPELLING TEST

SECTION A: SCORECARD

Congratulations! You have completed the 10-minute tests!

How did you do? Enter your score for each test in the grid below:

TEST	SCORE
Grammar and Punctuation Test 1	
Grammar and Punctuation Test 2	
Grammar and Punctuation Test 3	
Grammar and Punctuation Test 4	
Spelling Test	
TOTAL	**(out of 52)**

Now check out the advice below and count your lucky stars!

0–17 marks	Well done for giving it a try! Try covering over your marks and giving the 10-minute tests another go. Practice makes perfect!	
18–35 marks	Great progress! Go back to the questions you found tricky and make sure you understand the answers. Then move on to the 20-minute tests!	
36–52 marks	Fantastic – amazing work! You have conquered this section and you can move straight on to the 20-minute tests!	

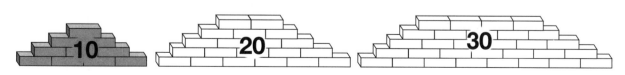

1 Draw a line to match each word with the correct **word class**.
Use each word class **once**.

Word	Word class
imagination	verb
imagine	adjective
imaginatively	noun
imaginative	adverb

1 mark

2 Which **punctuation mark** is used in the following sentence, not including the full stop?

Lucas was feeling tired – he decided not to go to volleyball practice.

Tick **one**.

a hyphen ⬜

a semi-colon ⬜

a dash ⬜

inverted commas ⬜

1 mark

3 Draw a line to match each sentence to its **function**.

Sentence		Function
Don't open the window		question
How brilliant this game is		statement
Do you like carrots or not		command
Jenna isn't coming to the barbecue		exclamation

1 mark

4 Read the sentence below. Which **word class** does each underlined word belong to? Write **N** for noun, **V** for verb or **A** for adjective in the boxes.

The <u>happy</u> old <u>woman</u> <u>sat</u> in her <u>comfy</u> chair.

1 mark

5 Identify **all** of the **punctuation marks** which are used in the text below. Tick the boxes.

Prisha stood at the edge of the cliff: it was a long way down.
She remembered being here once before; she liked it then, too.

bracket ☐   comma ☐   exclamation mark ☐

colon ☐   full stop ☐   semi-colon ☐

1 mark

6 Circle the **adverbial phrase** in this sentence.

I'm so tired because I've been playing football since three o'clock.

1 mark

7 Which **prefix** can be added to all of the words below?

septic

social

clockwise

freeze

Tick **one**.

super- ☐

anti- ☐

auto- ☐

inter- ☐

1 mark

8 Complete the sentences below using appropriate **pronouns**.

Olly didn't feel like doing his homework. It was science and he found

_____ difficult. His friends were good at science, though.

Maybe _____ could help him, he thought.

1 mark

9 Read the sentences below. Which **tenses** are used?
Tick **one** for each sentence.

	Past simple	Present simple	Present perfect	Future simple
It took several hours until the traffic jam cleared.				
I don't know whether to go to the barbecue or not.				
I'll be at my cousin's house all day on Saturday.				
I've never tried Turkish food.				

1 mark

10 Which **relative pronoun** is missing from the sentence below?

Where's the book _____ I lent you?

Tick **one**.

what ☐

whose ☐

that ☐

who ☐

1 mark

11

Draw a line to match each **question** with the correct **question tag**.
Use each question tag **once**.

Question   **Question tag**

You've eaten all the cake,   didn't you?

You left your muddy boots outside,   weren't you?

You were late for your bus,   haven't you?

1 mark

12

Which sentence is the most **formal**?

Tick **one**.

Pass me the salt, please.   ⬜

How's it going?   ⬜

Would you be interested in accompanying me to
the football match?   ⬜

Do you want to come over and try out my new video game?   ⬜

1 mark

13

Insert a pair of **brackets** in the correct place in the sentence below.

The neighbour's dog the big white one, not the little brown one is

always in our garden!

1 mark

14 Circle **all** the **synonyms** of the word *mischievous*.

good   harmless

playful   naughty

well-behaved   disobedient

1 mark

15 Which of these sentences uses the correct **punctuation**?

Tick **one**.

"I don't know where your coat is! It'll be wherever you left it," said Dad. ☐

"I don't know where your coat is, it'll be wherever you left it," said Dad. ☐

"I don't know where you coat is. It'll be wherever you left it", said Dad. ☐

I don't know where your coat is. "It'll be wherever you left it," said Dad. ☐

1 mark

16 Add the missing **punctuation** to the sentence below.

I'm not keen on vegetables, are you

1 mark

17 What is the word in bold an example of in the following sentence?

If I **were** you, I'd stay in bed and call the doctor.

Tick **one**.

the passive ☐

the past simple ☐

the subjunctive ☐

the present perfect ☐

1 mark

18 How many types of object does Zara collect?

Zara loves collecting gold paper and clips.

Tick **one**.

two ☐

three ☐

1 mark

19 Draw a line to match each sentence which contains an **apostrophe** to what it shows.

Sentence

That's my skateboard.

Is this your son's coat?

Where is your grandparents' house?

What it shows

plural possession

contracted form

singular possession

1 mark

20 Look at the sentences below. Write a **noun**, a **verb** or an **adjective** in each sentence, using the root word *solve*.

Salt will _____ in hot water. The grains disappear

completely.

Sugar is _____ in hot water, too.

We need to find a _____ to the problem. Then

everything will be OK!

_____
1 mark

Well done for completing this test! Add up your marks and work out your total score.

TOTAL SCORE: .... (out of 20)

GRAMMAR AND PUNCTUATION
TEST 2

1 Circle the correct **plural suffix** of each word below.

wish   -s / -es

judge   -s / -es

message   -s / -es

length   -s / -es

_____
1 mark

2 Which sentence is an **exclamation**?

Tick **one**.

Go and see that movie ☐

What an awesome movie that was ☐

Abi told me how awesome the movie was ☐

Have you seen the movie yet ☐

_____
1 mark

3 Circle the correct **subordinating conjunction** in the sentence below.

I never lend my brother my things **if** / **when** / **that** / **because** he never gives them back!

_____
1 mark

4 What kind of **parenthesis** does this sentence show?

My sister – the older one – gave me this necklace for my birthday.

Tick **one**.

brackets ☐

dashes ☐

commas ☐

1 mark

5 Circle the **object** in this sentence.

I've just finished reading a really interesting book.

1 mark

6 In which sentence are the **colons** and **semi-colons** used correctly?

Tick **one**.

We've done some interesting things in science: classifying living things; what fossils can tell us; and how light travels. ☐

We've done some interesting things in science; classifying living things: what fossils can tell us: and how light travels. ☐

We've done some interesting things: in science; classifying living things; what fossils can tell us; and how light travels. ☐

1 mark

7 Circle the **three synonyms** below.

talk ask speak chat

1 mark

8 Which sentence uses **capital letters** correctly?

Tick **one**.

Let's go and see big Ben! It's next to the river Thames in an area called westminster. ☐

Let's go and see Big Ben! It's next to the River Thames in an area called Westminster. ☐

Let's go and see Big Ben! It's next to the river Thames in an area called Westminster. ☐

1 mark

9 Which sentence is written in **Standard English**?

Tick **one**.

I ain't going to Joe's party cos I'm too busy. ☐

Bethany was unsure about going to Joe's party because she was busy. ☐

Bethany done her homework before she went to Joe's party. ☐

1 mark

10 Which sentence containing a **modal verb** is the **least** certain to happen?

Tick **one**.

I'll finish my geography project when I get back from Grandma's. ☐

Shona said she might come round later when she's had her dinner. ☐

We must tidy our bedrooms or we'll get told off again! ☐

1 mark

11 Which sentence uses the **apostrophe** correctly?
Tick **one** box in each row.

Sentence	Apostrophe(s) used correctly	Apostrophe(s) used incorrectly
Jack's apple is red but Olivia's is green.		
Seren's favourite fruits are apples and oranges.		
I love apple's, orange's and pear's.		
The apples' on our tree are green and red.		

1 mark

12 Complete the sentence below with a **possessive pronoun**.

This game doesn't belong to me. It belongs to those children.

It's _____.

1 mark

13 Add **bullet points** to this list in the correct places.

Equipment you will need for the experiment:

a paperclip

a bowl of water

a coin.

Now follow the instructions and watch the items float!

1 mark

14 What is the **function** of the sentence below?

Switch the light off when you've finished in the bathroom

Tick **one**.

statement	☐
question	☐
exclamation	☐
command	☐

1 mark

15 Are these sentences **active** or **passive**?
Tick active or passive for each sentence.

	Active	Passive
A warning was issued that there may be a hurricane on its way.		
I've just had my first ever snowboarding lesson.		
These posters were designed by my friends Jess and Will.		
We did some research into the Ancient Egyptians.		

_____
1 mark

16 Write **two apostrophes** in the sentences below.

The childrens games were very entertaining.

Daniels game was the best.

_____
1 mark

17 Are these **tenses** correct or incorrect?
Write ✓ for correct and ✗ for incorrect.

Ahmed's just had his hair cut.   _____

I wrote twenty emails since nine o'clock.   _____

Did you do your homework already?   _____

Have you washed the dishes yet?   _____

1 mark

18 Where should the **hyphen** go? Tick **one**.

The Venus flytrap is an insect eating plant.

1 mark

19 Circle the correct **verb forms** in the text below.

Mikey never wants to **come** / **came** to the park these days. He was

brilliant at skateboarding but then he **fallen** / **fell** off his board and

hurt his ankle. I **is** / **am** going to remind him how brilliant he was!

1 mark

20 Change the **nouns** to **adjectives**.

Noun		Adjective
adventure	→	_____
danger	→	_____
passion	→	_____
confidence	→	_____

1 mark

Well done for completing this test! Add up your marks and work out your total score.

TOTAL SCORE: .... (out of 20)

1 Circle the correct **conjunctions**.

Emily hasn't told me whether **and** / **or** / **but** not she's coming

to the beach on Saturday. I don't mind **and** / **or** / **but** if she

doesn't let me know soon, I'll ask someone else **and** / **or** / **but**

there won't be space in the car for her any more.

1 mark

2 Circle the **comma** which is **not** needed in this sentence.

I don't know whether to go to Tom's house, watch a film,

go for a nap, or read my book!

1 mark

3 Draw a line to match each sentence to its **function**.

Sentence	**Function**
I've been looking forward to the concert for ages	exclamation
What an amazing time we had at the concert	question
Are you thinking of going to the concert this evening	command
Go now or you'll be late for the concert	statement

1 mark

4 Which of the following sentences need **questions marks**?

Tick **three**.

Could you tell me what time the next train is, please ☐

They didn't seem to know what time the next train was ☐

This is the train to Paris, isn't it ☐

Which of the trains is direct ☐

1 mark

5 Write **subject** or **object** in the boxes below.

Joseph ate an enormous burger.

↑   ↑

[   ]   [   ]

1 mark

6 Write a **relative pronoun** in the sentence below.

My cousin, _____ lives in Sydney, has invited me to go and visit

him this summer.

1 mark

7 Complete this sentence with the correct **question tag**.

You've never been to Asia, _____ you?

1 mark

8 What is the meaning of this **hyphenated** sentence?

That's a man-eating bear over there!

Tick **one**.

There is a man who is eating some bears. ☐

There is a bear which eats people. ☐

1 mark

SPELLING TEST SCRIPTS

Instructions for parents, carers and teachers

This pullout section contains the scripts for all the spelling tests. Remove this section and keep it in a safe place. You will need it whenever you use one of the spelling tests. To administer a spelling test, read out these instructions:

- *Look at your copy of the spelling test. There are twelve/twenty sentences. Each sentence has a word missing. The missing word is shown by a line.*

- *I am going to read each sentence in turn. Listen carefully to the missing word and write this on the line, making sure you spell it correctly.*

- *First I will read the word, then I will read the word within the sentence, and then I will repeat the word.*

- *Do you have any questions?*

Once you have answered any questions, read aloud the spelling test script on the following pages.

Use the following format to read out each sentence:

> *The word is **friend**.*
>
> *My best **friend** Connor is really good at gymnastics.*
>
> *The word is **friend**.*

Give children as much time as they need to write each spelling word before going on to the next question.

If children are unsure how to spell a word, encourage them to have a go.

At the end of the test, read all the sentences again. Give children the opportunity to make any changes they wish to their answers.

When the spelling test has been completed, mark it together.

Audio files for each of the spelling tests can also be downloaded at
www.yorknotes.com/primary/ks2/english/tests

SECTION A – SPELLING TEST

1 My best **friend** Connor is really good at gymnastics.

2 I love **mystery** stories – you never know what will happen!

3 We had **trouble** getting tickets for the match.

4 "**Actually**, my name's Tegan, not Joanna," said the girl.

5 The pirates found the **treasure** on the beach.

6 Hannah got her favourite footballer's **autograph** after the match.

7 For the special **occasion** Sonja bought a new dress.

8 The teacher gave an **explanation** of the solar system.

9 Luke was **conscious** that he was looking quite scruffy.

10 My **neighbour** is having a party at the weekend.

11 Scientists wonder about the **existence** of life on other planets.

12 The **referee** ran backwards and forwards along the pitch.

SECTION B – SPELLING TEST

1 That cake looks delicious – can I have a **piece**, please?

2 That's a **beautiful** drawing, Anya.

3 Your **tongue** has turned blue from those sweets you ate!

4 I loved that **scene** with the ugly purple alien.

5 "Does anyone have any **questions**?" asked the teacher.

6 That photocopy **machine** is so noisy!

7 I **doubt** if we will reach the station in time.

8 Mum got some medicine from the **chemist** for me.

9 Is that your next-door **neighbour** over there?

10 Amir lives in a **mountainous** region of his country.

11 "I'm sorry but I've **forgotten** my homework," said Freddie.

12 Jack was **disappointed** that his friends couldn't play outside.

13 They rowed out to the **island** in a boat.

14 The police did a **thorough** search of the area.

15 Jon didn't **receive** the text I sent him.

16 This ring contains **precious** stones as well as gold.

17 You're being more of a **hindrance** than a help!

18 Emma **practises** the guitar every day and she's improving.

19 Protective clothing is **essential** for factory workers.

20 Are there any tickets still **available** for the concert?

SECTION C – SPELLING TEST 1

1 Have you eaten the **whole** cake?

2 Please don't **touch** the exhibits on display.

3 "How much do you **weigh**?" asked the doctor.

4 I would have **preferred** to go shopping with you.

5 These tiny **creatures** are called tree frogs.

6 Billy's parents have got an **antiques** shop in town.

7 The pupils **interact** well with each other in class.

8 We've been learning about the ancient **pyramids** in Egypt.

9 There was some **confusion** when the fire alarm sounded.

10 Please don't leave any personal **possessions** on the bus.

11 Will you make a **donation** to the charity, please?

12 Sophie **accidentally** stood on the cat's tail.

13 That's the **toughest** mountain we've ever climbed!

14 On my bedroom **ceiling** there are some glow-in-the-dark stars.

15 It's become **apparent** that someone's been leaving the computers on.

16 The **principal** dancer came on stage and everyone cheered.

17 I think **artificial** intelligence will replace teachers eventually!

18 My sister's **ambitious** – she wants to be an astronaut.

19 A **parliament** is a group of people who make laws.

20 This soup is **incredibly** salty – ugh!

SECTION C – SPELLING TEST 2

1 Mmm, this pizza's **great** – thanks, Dad!

2 Li looked **through** the keyhole to see who was home.

3 They must have a new **chef** at the café.

4 Ouch! There's a great big **knot** in my hair!

5 The audience **groaned** because the joke was so bad.

6 I don't understand what this mathematical **symbol** means.

7 "It's been a **pleasure** to meet you," he said.

8 You have to **obey** the rules at school.

9 Pins and needles is a weird **sensation**, isn't it?

10 Gemma lives in an **enormous** house near the park.

11 My cousin will be a famous **musician** one day.

12 The handwriting on this letter is **illegible** – who's it for?

13 Thanks for making my birthday party so **special**, everyone.

14 Are you trying to **deceive** me?

15 You've got great **rhythm**; you can feel the music!

16 My **stomach** hurts – I've eaten too much!

17 They're **transferring** our best player to another team.

18 What are the most **nutritious** foods for humans?

19 In case of **emergency** use the fire escape.

20 The trees have grown **considerably** in the last few years.

9 Which **bulleted list** uses the correct punctuation? Tick **one**.

What you need for the trip:

- picnic lunch

- comfortable clothing

- waterproof boots ☐

- What you need for the trip

- picnic lunch

- comfortable clothing

- waterproof boots ☐

1 mark

10 Circle the **formal** word or phrase in each pair.

ask / request   talk about / discuss

obtain / get   apologise / say sorry

1 mark

11 Which **punctuation mark** should be used in the place shown by the arrow?

How beautiful that sunset is

↑

Tick **one**.

comma ☐

question mark ☐

exclamation mark ☐

full stop ☐

1 mark

12 Circle the **relative clause** in the sentence below.

Jacob, whose father works in a chocolate factory, gets lots of free

chocolate bars: he often gives me some, too.

1 mark

13 Read the sentence with the **fronted adverbial** below.
Insert a **comma** in the correct place.

The day after tomorrow we're going on holiday.

1 mark

14 Circle the **subordinate clause** in this sentence:

Although we were scared, we still went on the fastest ride.

1 mark

15 Which sentence uses the **present perfect tense**?

Tick **one**.

The whistle blew and the match began. ☐

The players were running around but no one was trying to score. ☐

Three players have been sent off so far in this game. ☐

My team scored the winning goal – it was a brilliant result! ☐

1 mark

16 Copy the sentence below. Write four **punctuation marks** in the sentence.

Sam said I have no idea who smashed the window

_____

_____

1 mark

17 Are the sentences below in the **passive** or **active voice**?
Write **P** for passive or **A** for active.

We were beaten by the other team 3–0. _____

The referee sent one of our players off. _____

Are you playing in tomorrow's match? _____

The winner of the cup will be announced soon. _____

1 mark

18 Write the correct word from the **word family** in the sentence below.

| medicine | medicate | medicinal | medical | medication |

You can _____ yourself against colds without going

to the doctor.

1 mark

19 What type of punctuation is shown in the sentence below?

The castle, which we'd never been to before, was full of interesting towers and corridors.

Tick **one**.

parenthesis ⬜

ellipsis ⬜

colon ⬜

1 mark

20 Make nouns by adding **-ness** or **-er**.
Make other changes to the word if necessary.

babysit → _____ (a person who looks after children)

shy → _____ (if you're shy, you suffer from this)

happy → _____ (the state of feeling happy)

win → _____ (someone who wins something)

1 mark

Well done for completing this test! Add up your marks and work out your total score.

TOTAL SCORE: ……………………… (out of 20)

SPELLING TEST

1 That cake looks delicious – can I have a _____, please?

2 That's a _____ drawing, Anya.

3 Your _____ has turned blue from those sweets you ate!

4 I loved that _____ with the ugly purple alien.

5 "Does anyone have any _____?" asked the teacher.

6 That photocopy _____ is so noisy!

7 I _____ if we will reach the station in time.

8 Mum got some medicine from the _____ for me.

9 Is that your next-door _____ over there?

10 Amir lives in a _____ region of his country.

11 "I'm sorry but I've _____ my homework," said Freddie.

12 Jack was _____ that his friends couldn't play outside.

13 They rowed out to the _____ in a boat.

14 The police did a _____ search of the area.

15 Jon didn't _____ the text I sent him.

16 This ring contains _____ stones as well as gold.

17 You're being more of a _____ than a help!

18 Emma _____ the guitar every day and she's improving.

19 Protective clothing is _____ for factory workers.

20 Are there any tickets still _____ for the concert?

Well done for completing this test! Add up your marks and work out your total score.

TOTAL SCORE: .... (out of 20)

SECTION B: SCORECARD

Congratulations! You have completed the 20-minute tests!

How did you do? Enter your score for each test in the grid below:

TEST	SCORE
Grammar and Punctuation Test 1	
Grammar and Punctuation Test 2	
Grammar and Punctuation Test 3	
Spelling Test	
TOTAL	**(out of 80)**

Now check out the advice below and count your lucky stars!

0–26 marks	Well done for giving it a try! Try covering over your marks and giving the 20-minute tests another go. Practice makes perfect!	⭐
27–53 marks	Great progress! Go back to the questions you found tricky and make sure you understand the answers. Then move on to the 30-minute tests!	⭐⭐
54–80 marks	Fantastic – amazing work! You have conquered this section and you can move straight on to the 30-minute tests!	⭐⭐⭐

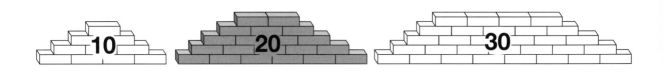

SECTION C: 30-MINUTE TESTS
GRAMMAR AND PUNCTUATION TEST

1 Which of the following words need **capital letters**?

Tick **two**.

peter ☐

dinosaur ☐

wednesday ☐

jelly ☐

1 mark

2 Look at the **adverbs** in the sentences below.
Tick the sentence which is **most certain**.

Tick **one**.

I'll probably go to visit Grandma after school. ☐

I'll definitely go to visit Grandma after school. ☐

Perhaps I'll go to visit Grandma after school. ☐

1 mark

3 Draw a line to match each sentence to its **function**.

Sentence	Function
I prefer doing arts and crafts to playing sport	exclamation
Do you like doing arts and crafts or do you prefer sport	statement
How completely boring drawing pictures is	command
Listen carefully and I'll tell you what we're doing in our art lesson today	question

1 mark

4 Which **possessive pronoun** correctly completes the first sentence below?

Those books aren't _____. They belong to us.

Tick **one**.

they ☐

them ☐

their ☐

theirs ☐

1 mark

SECTION C: GRAMMAR AND PUNCTUATION TEST

5

What do the following **prefixes** mean?
Draw lines to match the prefixes with their meanings.

Prefix	Meaning
super-	against
anti-	self or by itself
auto-	above, over, beyond

1 mark

6

Circle the correct **subordinating conjunction** to complete this sentence.

Because / **If** / **Although** Carrie wasn't feeling very confident, she gave a brilliant talk in class.

1 mark

7 Read the sentence below and think about its **function**.
Tick **one** piece of advice you should give about punctuation.

What an absolutely beautiful day it is

Tick **one**.

There should be an exclamation mark at the end. ☐

There should be a question mark at the end. ☐

There should be a full stop at the end. ☐

1 mark

8 Circle the **adverbial phrase** in the sentence below.

He didn't stop running until he was exhausted.

1 mark

9 Which of these sentences would be most appropriate for a **formal** letter?

Tick **one**.

I want to find out about the summer camp
in America. ☐

What about the summer camp in America? ☐

I would like to enquire about the summer
camp in America. ☐

Can you tell me about the summer camp
in America? ☐

1 mark

10

Are the words in bold **nouns** or **verbs**?
Write **N** for **noun** or **V** for **verb** on the lines.

We'd better get to football **practice** – we're already late.   _____

Whatever you decide to do, it makes no **difference** to me.   _____

You should **exercise** a little every day.   _____

Can you **balance** on one leg?   _____

1 mark

11

Circle the **adverb** in the sentence below.

The children were yawning loudly, so their parents decided to take

them home.

1 mark

12

Where should the **dash** go in the sentence below? Tick **one**.

Quick, let's go the bus is coming right now!

1 mark

13 Complete the sentence with a **conjunction**.

Benjy listened to music _____ he waited for his friend.

1 mark

14 Which sentence uses the **colon** correctly?

Tick **one**.

Look! There's Susan over there, she's had:
her hair cut really short! ☐

Look! There's Susan: over there, she's had
her hair cut really short! ☐

Look! There's Susan, over there: she's had
her hair cut really short! ☐

Look! There's Susan over there, she's had
her hair cut: really short! ☐

1 mark

15 Circle the **expanded noun phrase** in one of the sentences below.

The Loch Ness Monster is a mythical water beast. It lives

in Scotland.

1 mark

16 Write the **root word** of the **word family** below.

heard   mishear   overheard   hearing

Root word: _____

1 mark

17 Which **verb form** completes the sentence below?

Alex _____ about the weird dream he'd had for a long time.

Tick **one**.

hasn't thought   ☐

doesn't think   ☐

hadn't thought   ☐

1 mark

18 Which set of **brackets** is **not** needed in the sentences below?
Circle the brackets.

Jenny (who I met in the first year) is my best friend. She loves

animals and she's got a dog (who's getting a bit old now), two cats

and a pet (snake).

1 mark

19 Which of these sentences uses the **subjunctive**?

Tick **one**.

I don't know about you, but I don't really enjoy acting. ☐

I've never met anyone who's as good an actor as Sandra. ☐

If Mrs Foley were to organise the school play, it would
be brilliant. ☐

_____
1 mark

20 What is the **ellipsis** doing in the sentence below?

Megan wasn't expecting the knock at the door. She opened it slowly and
there on the doorstep was ... a golden envelope.

Tick **one**.

showing that a word is missing ☐

indicating a pause in speech ☐

creating suspense ☐

_____
1 mark

21 Look at these words with **suffixes**. Which are spelled correctly?

Tick **two**.

apologyse ☐

oxygenate ☐

simplify ☐

activeate ☐

_____
1 mark

22

Rearrange the words in the sentence below to make it a **question**.
Use only the given words. Remember to punctuate your sentence correctly.

Statement: The park is closed today.

Question: _____

_____

1 mark

23

Circle the **modal verb** in each sentence.

You should tell the teacher what's happened.

You must be quiet when the teacher's speaking.

You ought to ask the teacher if there's anything you

don't understand.

You could talk to the teacher about what's worrying

you.

1 mark

24 Complete the sentences with the correct **verb forms** of the verbs in the boxes.

I have never _____ such an strange-looking animal before.

↑

to see

I wonder what it _____.

↑

to be

1 mark

25 Which sentences use **exclamation marks** correctly?

Tick **two**.

What a brilliant story! ☐

How are you feeling today! ☐

Is that a tiger with its cubs! ☐

How cute that puppy is! ☐

1 mark

26 Complete the sentence with the correct **progressive** form of the verb in brackets.

The pupils _____ (have) fun in the playground

when the teacher called them inside.

1 mark

27 Copy the text below. Create **three** sentences by including **full stops** and **capital letters**.

Colm never went out without his phone today, he'd forgotten it now he wouldn't be able to find out where his friend had gone.

_____

_____

_____

1 mark

28 Write **apostrophes** in the sentence below.

I cant go to the cinema tonight because its my Mums birthday and were going out for a meal.

1 mark

29 Add two **semi-colons** to the sentence below.

I love art classes at school. We've studied great artists and designers improved our painting, drawing and sculpture techniques and created sketchbooks to record our observations.

1 mark

SECTION C: GRAMMAR AND PUNCTUATION TEST   65

30 Rewrite the underlined parts of the sentence below in the **passive voice**.

They make cola in the USA, but people drink it all over the world.

_____

_____

1 mark

Well done for completing this test! Add up your marks and work out your total score.

TOTAL SCORE: .... (out of 30)

SECTION C:TEST

SPELLING TEST 1

This test should take you 15 minutes.
Take Spelling Tests 1 and 2 together for a 30-minute test!

1 Have you eaten the _____ cake?

2 Please don't _____ the exhibits on display.

3 "How much do you _____?" asked the doctor.

4 I would have _____ to go shopping with you.

5 These tiny _____ are called tree frogs.

6 Billy's parents have got an _____ shop in town.

7 The pupils _____ well with each other in class.

8 We've been learning about the ancient _____ in Egypt.

9 There was some _____ when the fire alarm sounded.

10 Please don't leave any personal _____ on the bus.

11 Will you make a _____ to the charity, please?

12 Sophie _____ stood on the cat's tail.

13 That's the _____ mountain we've ever climbed!

14 On my bedroom _____ there are some glow-in-the-dark stars.

15 It's become _____ that someone's been leaving the

computers on.

16 The _____ dancer came on stage and everyone cheered.

17 I think _____ intelligence will replace teachers eventually!

18 My sister's _____ – she wants to be an astronaut.

19 A _____ is a group of people who make laws.

20 This soup is _____ salty – ugh!

Well done for completing this test! Add up your marks and work out your total score.

TOTAL SCORE: .... (out of 20)

SPELLING TEST 2

1 Mmm, this pizza's _____ – thanks, Dad!

2 Li looked _____ the keyhole to see who was home.

3 They must have a new _____ at the café.

4 Ouch! There's a great big _____ in my hair!

5 The audience _____ because the joke was so bad.

6 I don't understand what this mathematical _____ means.

7 "It's been a _____ to meet you," he said.

8 You have to _____ the rules at school.

9 Pins and needles is a weird _____, isn't it?

10 Gemma lives in an _____ house near the park.

11 My cousin will be a famous _____ one day.

12 The handwriting on this letter is _____ – who's it for?

13 Thanks for making my birthday party so _____, everyone.

14 Are you trying to _____ me?

15 You've got great _____; you can feel the music!

16 My _____ hurts – I've eaten too much!

17 They're _____ our best player to another team.

SECTION C: SPELLING TEST 2   69

18 What are the most _____ foods for humans?

19 In case of _____ use the fire escape.

20 The trees have grown _____ in the last few years.

Well done for completing this test! Add up your marks and work out your total score.

TOTAL SCORE: ……………………….. (out of 20)

Congratulations! You have completed the 30-minute tests!

How did you do? Enter your score for each test in the grid below:

TEST	SCORE
Grammar and Punctuation Test	
Spelling Test 1	
Spelling Test 2	
TOTAL	**(out of 70)**

Now check out the advice below and count your lucky stars!

0–23 marks	Well done for giving it a try! Try covering over your marks and giving the 30-minute test another go. Practice makes perfect!	⭐
24–47 marks	Great progress! Go back to the questions you found tricky and make sure you understand the answers.	⭐⭐
48–70 marks	Fantastic – amazing work! You have conquered this section.	⭐⭐⭐

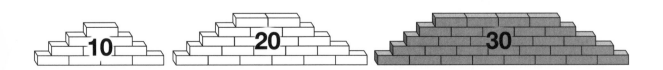

GRAMMAR AND PUNCTUATION TEST 1

1. 1 mark

On Tuesday James and I went swimming at the new pool in the centre of London.

2. 1 mark

Exclamation

3. 1 mark for all three correct

My friend Mike always **comes** round to my house on Friday nights. We **watch** a film or **play** computer games.

4. 1 mark for all three correct

I told Dad I'd ring him **when** football practice finished, **so** he could come **and** pick me up.

5. 1 mark for both correct

By the time Dad got home from work, we'd already eaten our dinner.

The school bus usually picks us up at about ten past eight.

6. 1 mark

My favourite snacks are chocolate, crisps, nuts and ice cream.

7. 1 mark for all three correct

It took ages to find **a** good place to have **the** picnic, but eventually we found **an** old wall to sit on.

8. 1 mark for all three correct

The girls, **who** go to dance class together every Saturday, became great friends.

I'm going to have a strawberry ice cream, **which** is my favourite flavour.

That's the boy **whose** father was a famous rock star in the 1990s.

9. 1 mark for all four correct

lucky	→	unfortunate
special	→	ordinary
generous	→	mean

10. 1 mark for both apostrophes correctly placed

This is Arjun's poster and those are the other students' posters.

GRAMMAR AND PUNCTUATION TEST 2

1. 1 mark for all three correct

What an amazing house ➜ !

Our house isn't very big ➜ .

Has your house got a garden ➜ ?

2. 1 mark

command

3. 1 mark

soon

4. 1 mark for both correct

I **play** netball with my friends on Saturdays and **visit** my grandparents on Sundays.

5. 1 mark

I was playing in the garden when Mum called me in for dinner.

6. 1 mark

Poppy didn't get home until late(;) her bus didn't turn up on time. She had two options: start walking or wait. She decided to wait and then three buses all came at once!

7. 1 mark

un-

8. 1 mark

Ben's new dog, which his family brought home at the weekend, has settled in well.

9. 1 mark

Noun phrase: The lazy old cat

10. 1 mark for all three correct

Sorry I **was** not at home when you called yesterday. I **was** out with my parents. We **were** at the supermarket for hours!

GRAMMAR AND PUNCTUATION TEST 3

1. 1 mark

bullet points

2. 1 mark

Subject: Maria

3. 1 mark

Subordinate clause: which were sitting neatly wrapped on the table

4. 1 mark

My dad often works shifts which last 24 hours.

5. 1 mark

full stop

6. 1 mark for all three correct

	Certain	Not certain
I might go to Jude's party at the weekend.		✓
Isaac will meet you at the corner in ten minutes.	✓	
It may rain later so take an umbrella with you.		✓

7. 1 mark

Words in brackets: Star Brand

8. 1 mark for all four correct

ill	→	-ness
end	→	-less
mouth	→	-ful
secret	→	-ly

9. 1 mark

Have you ever been to Thornly theme park?

10. 1 mark for all three correct

a. Do you know **whose** bag that is? Is it Charlotte's?

b. Do you mean the one **which** is hanging on the back of the chair? Sorry, I don't know **who** it belongs to.

GRAMMAR AND PUNCTUATION TEST 4

1. 1 mark

question

2. 1 mark

I bought a lot of snacks to eat during the film: popcorn, sweets and nachos – Mum said I was greedy!

3. 1 mark for all three correct

After swimming, we had a milkshake **at** the café **before** we went home.

4. 1 mark

The red car is ours.

5. 1 mark for all four correct

playful

homeless

endless

wonderful

6. 1 mark for either answer

Incorrect verb form: have *or* have got

7. 1 mark for both correct

Erin (my older sister) is really good on the guitar.

The cake – which looked great – wasn't as tasty as I'd hoped.

8. 1 mark for both correct

Subordinate clause: After we've been to the cinema

Main clause: Dad's going to take us for a pizza.

9. 1 mark for all four correct

"I don't know where your glasses are," said Jo.

10. 1 mark for all three correct

I'm sitting by my bedroom window, and I can see our neighbours in their garden. Their little boy, Jules, **is playing** with a ball and his parents **are reading**.

SPELLING TEST

1 mark for each correct answer

1. friend

2. mystery

3. trouble

4. Actually

5. treasure

6. autograph

7. occasion

8. explanation

9. conscious

10. neighbour

11. existence

12. referee

SECTION A: ANSWERS

GRAMMAR AND PUNCTUATION TEST 1

1. 1 mark for all four correct

imagination	→	noun
imagine	→	verb
imaginatively	→	adverb
imaginative	→	adjective

2. 1 mark

a dash

3. 1 mark for all four correct

Don't open the window → command

How brilliant this game is → exclamation

Do you like carrots or not → question

Jenna isn't coming to the barbecue → statement

4. 1 mark for all four correct

happy and comfy: adjectives

woman: noun

sat: verb

5. 1 mark for all four correct

colon, comma, full stop, semi-colon

6. 1 mark

Adverbial phrase: since three o'clock

7. 1 mark

anti-

8. 1 mark for both correct

Olly didn't feel like doing his homework. It was science and he found **it** difficult. His friends were good at science, though. Maybe **they** could help him, he thought.

9. 1 mark for all four correct

	Past simple	Present simple	Present perfect	Future simple
It took several hours until the traffic jam cleared.	✓			
I don't know whether to go to the barbecue or not.		✓		
I'll be at my cousin's house all day on Saturday.				✓
I've never tried Turkish food.			✓	

10. 1 mark

that

11. 1 mark for all three correct

You've eaten all the cake,	→	haven't you?
You left your muddy boots outside,	→	didn't you?
You were late for your bus,	→	weren't you?

12. 1 mark

Would you be interested in accompanying me to the football match?

13. 1 mark

The neighbour's dog (the big white one, not the little brown one) is always in our garden!

14. 1 mark for all three correct

Synonyms: naughty, playful, disobedient

15. 1 mark

"I don't know where your coat is! It'll be wherever you left it," said Dad.

16. 1 mark

I'm not keen on vegetables, are you?

17. 1 mark

the subjunctive

18. 1 mark

two

19. 1 mark for all three correct

That's my skateboard.	→	contracted form
Is this your son's coat?	→	singular possession
Where is your grandparents' house?	→	plural possession

20. 1 mark for all three correct

Salt will **dissolve** in hot water. The grains disappear completely.

Sugar is **soluble** in hot water, too.

We need to find a **solution** to the problem. Then everything will be OK!

GRAMMAR AND PUNCTUATION TEST 2

1. 1 mark for all four correct

wish -es, judge -s, message -s, length -s

2. 1 mark

What an awesome movie that was

3. 1 mark

I never lend my brother my things **because** he never gives them back!

4. 1 mark

dashes

5. 1 mark for either answer

Object: book *or* a really interesting book

6. 1 mark

We've done some interesting things in science: classifying living things; what fossils can tell us; and how light travels.

7. 1 mark for all three correct

talk, speak, chat

8. 1 mark

Let's go and see Big Ben! It's next to the River Thames in an area called Westminster.

9. 1 mark

Bethany was unsure about going to Joe's party because she was busy.

10. 1 mark

Shona said she might come round later when she's had her dinner.

11. 1 mark for all four correct

Sentence	Apostrophe(s) used correctly	Apostrophe(s) used incorrectly
Jack's apple is red but Olivia's is green.	✓	
Seren's favourite fruits are apples and oranges.	✓	
I love apple's, orange's and pear's.		✓
The apples' on our tree are green and red.		✓

12. 1 mark

This game doesn't belong to me. It belongs to those children. It's **theirs**.

13. 1 mark for all three correct

Equipment you will need for the experiment:

• a paperclip

• a bowl of water

• a coin.

Now follow the instructions and watch the items float!

14. 1 mark

command

15. 1 mark for all four correct

	Active	Passive
A warning was issued that there may be a hurricane on its way.		✓
I've just had my first ever snowboarding lesson.	✓	
These posters were designed by my friends Jess and Will.		✓
We did some research into the Ancient Egyptians.	✓	

16. 1 mark for both correct

The **children's** games were very entertaining. **Daniel's** game was the best.

17. 1 mark for all four correct

Ahmed's just had his hair cut. ✓

I wrote twenty emails since nine o'clock. ✗

Did you do your homework already? ✗

Have you washed the dishes yet? ✓

18. 1 mark

The Venus flytrap is an insect-eating plant.

19. 1 mark for all three correct

Mikey never wants to **come** to the park these days. He was brilliant at skateboarding but then he **fell** off his board and hurt his ankle. I **am** going to remind him how brilliant he was!

20. 1 mark for all four correct

adventure	→	adventurous
danger	→	dangerous
passion	→	passionate
confidence	→	confident

GRAMMAR AND PUNCTUATION TEST 3

1. 1 mark for all three correct

Emily hasn't told me whether **or** not she's coming to the beach on Saturday. I don't mind **but** if she doesn't let me know soon, I'll ask someone else **and** there won't be space in the car for her any more.

2. 1 mark

I don't know whether to go to Tom's house, watch a film, go for a nap⊙ or read my book!

3. 1 mark for all four correct

I've been looking forward to the concert for ages	→	statement
What an amazing time we had at the concert	→	exclamation
Are you thinking of going to the concert this evening	→	question
Go now or you'll be late for the concert	→	command

4. 1 mark for all three correct

Could you tell me what time the next train is, please

This is the train to Paris, isn't it

Which of the trains is direct

5. 1 mark for both correct

Subject: Joseph, Object: burger

6. 1 mark

My cousin, **who** lives in Sydney, has invited me to go and visit him this summer.

7. 1 mark

You've never been to Asia, **have** you?

8. 1 mark

There is a bear which eats people.

9. 1 mark

What you need for the trip:

• picnic lunch

• comfortable clothing

• waterproof boots

10. 1 mark for all four correct

Formal words: request, discuss, obtain, apologise

11. 1 mark

exclamation mark

12. 1 mark

Relative clause: whose father works in a chocolate factory

13. 1 mark

The day after tomorrow, we're going on holiday.

14. 1 mark

Subordinate clause: Although we were scared

15. 1 mark

Three players have been sent off so far in this game.

16. 1 mark for all four correct

Sam said, "I have no idea who smashed the window."

17. 1 mark for all four correct

We were beaten by the other team 3-0.	P
The referee sent one of our players off.	A
Are you playing in tomorrow's match?	A
The winner of the cup will be announced soon.	P

18. 1 mark

You can **medicate** yourself against colds without going to the doctor.

19. 1 mark

parenthesis

20. 1 mark for all four correct

babysit	➜	babysitter
shy	➜	shyness
happy	➜	happiness
win	➜	winner

SPELLING TEST

1 mark for each correct answer.

1. piece	11. forgotten
2. beautiful	12. disappointed
3. tongue	13. island
4. scene	14. thorough
5. questions	15. receive
6. machine	16. precious
7. doubt	17. hindrance
8. chemist	18. practises
9. neighbour	19. essential
10. mountainous	20. available

GRAMMAR AND PUNCTUATION TEST

1. 1 mark for both correct

peter

wednesday

2. 1 mark

I'll definitely go to visit Grandma after school.

3. 1 mark for all four correct

I prefer doing arts and crafts to playing sport → statement

Do you like doing arts and crafts or do you prefer sport → question

How completely boring drawing pictures is → exclamation

Listen carefully and I'll tell you what we're doing in our art lesson today → command

4. 1 mark

Those books aren't **theirs**.
They belong to us.

5. 1 mark for all three correct

super- → above, over, beyond

anti- → against

auto- → self or by itself

6. 1 mark

Although Carrie wasn't feeling very confident, she gave a brilliant talk in class.

7. 1 mark

There should be an exclamation mark at the end.

8. 1 mark

Adverbial phrase: until he was exhausted.

9. 1 mark

I would like to enquire about the summer camp in America.

10. 1 mark for all four correct

We'd better get to football **practice** – we're already late.	Noun
Whatever you decide to do, it makes no **difference** to me.	Noun
You should **exercise** a little every day.	Verb
Can you **balance** on one leg?	Verb

11. 1 mark

The children were yawning **loudly**, so their parents decided to take them home.

12. 1 mark

Quick, let's go – the bus is coming right now!

13. 1 mark

Benjy listened to music **while/as/whilst** he waited for his friend.

14. 1 mark

Look! There's Susan, over there: she's had her hair cut really short!

15. 1 mark

The Loch Ness Monster is **a mythical water beast**. It lives in Scotland.

16. 1 mark

Root word: hear

17. 1 mark

hadn't thought

18. 1 mark

Brackets not needed: (snake)

19. 1 mark

If Mrs Foley were to organise the school play, it would be brilliant.

20. 1 mark

creating suspense

21. 1 mark for both correct

- oxygenate
- simplify

22. 1 mark

Question: Is the park closed today?

23. 1 mark for all four correct

You **should** tell the teacher what's happened.

You **must** be quiet when the teacher's speaking.

You **ought** to ask the teacher if there's anything you don't understand.

You **could** talk to the teacher about what's worrying you.

24. 1 mark for both correct

I have never **seen** such an strange-looking animal before. I wonder what it **is**.

25. 1 mark for both correct

What a brilliant story!

How cute that puppy is!

26. 1 mark for both words correct

The pupils **were having** fun in the playground when the teacher called them inside.

27. 1 mark for all four correct

Colm never went out without his phone. **T**oday, he'd forgotten it. **N**ow he wouldn't be able to find out where his friend had gone.

28. 1 mark for all four correct

I can't go to the cinema tonight because it's my Mum's birthday and we're going out for a meal.

29. 1 mark for both correct

I love art classes at school. We've studied great artists and designers; improved our painting, drawing and sculpture techniques; and created sketchbooks to record our observations.

30. 1 mark for both correct

Cola is made in the USA but it is drunk by people all over the world.

SPELLING TEST 1

1 mark for each correct answer

1. whole
2. touch
3. weigh
4. preferred
5. creatures
6. antiques
7. interact
8. pyramids
9. confusion
10. possessions
11. donation
12. accidentally
13. toughest
14. ceiling
15. apparent
16. principal
17. artificial
18. ambitious
19. parliament
20. incredibly

SPELLING TEST 2

1 mark for each correct answer

1. great
2. through
3. chef
4. knot
5. groaned
6. symbol
7. pleasure
8. obey
9. sensation
10. enormous
11. musician
12. illegible
13. special
14. deceive
15. rhythm
16. stomach
17. transferring
18. nutritious
19. emergency
20. considerably

RECORD YOUR PROGRESS!

Congratulations! You have completed all the tests!

How did you do overall? Enter your score for each test in the grid below, then add them together to reveal your Grand Total:

SECTION A: 10-Minute Tests

Grammar and Punctuation Test 1	
Grammar and Punctuation Test 2	
Grammar and Punctuation Test 3	
Grammar and Punctuation Test 4	
Spelling Test	
TOTAL	

SECTION B: 20-Minute Tests

Grammar and Punctuation Test 1	
Grammar and Punctuation Test 2	
Grammar and Punctuation Test 3	
Spelling Test	
TOTAL	

SECTION C: 30-Minute Tests

Grammar and Punctuation Test	
Spelling Test 1	
Spelling Test 2	
TOTAL	

GRAND TOTAL: .... (out of 202)

Now check out the advice below and count your awards!

0–67 marks	You're getting there! Find the tests that you found hardest and give them another go – with a little practice your skills will improve!	
68–135 marks	Great progress! Re-read any questions you found trickier than others – can you improve your marks this time?	
136–202 marks	Fantastic – amazing reading skills! Why not try re-taking the tests just before your SATs to make sure you're on top?